Adriana Silvestri

Magic moments in
FLORENCE

Mandragora

©1999 **La Mandragora** srl
50122 Firenze, piazza Duomo 9
www.mandragora.it

Edited by *Alberto Anichini, Sandra Rosi*

ISBN 88-85957-29-3

Printed in Italy - *Alpilito Firenze*

Introduction

During the 18th and 19th centuries travellers who visited Florence - an obligatory port of call on the Grand Tour - often included in their travel diaries sketches and drawings which, more than any amount of writing, often succeeded in capturing a fleeting, intense image, an unusual or curious feature, or abrupt and revealing contrast between the relics of history and daily reality.

In many ways this too is a travel diary. With a difference compared to its forerunners: it reflects many visits I have made to the city, at different times and in different moods. The overall impression, therefore, is that of a continual internal evocation and renewal of scenes and things observed; the result of that 'happy nostalgia' which helps us to appreciate the profound significance and the profound link - imperceptible on that first eager, but obviously superficial visit - that exists between a museum and a market, a church and a designer boutique, a cloister and a wine shop.

This kind of association can lead far afield: Palazzo Pitti brought to mind not only the image of Eleonora di Toledo, wife of Cosimo I, but also the precious fabrics which the beautiful wife of the first grand duke so loved; Palazzo Davanzati lead me to consider the sophisticated food of the period and the jovial ritual of the banquet. The same is true of the famous and less famous characters portrayed in the Uffizi - sometimes I amused myself altering their costume or imagined them facing each other to have a chat.

Almost always I worked on the spot: sometimes amidst a crowd, sometimes in quiet corners enlivened by subdued laughter or quick footsteps, inside and outside churches, in squares and courtyards. Always with much pleasure, however, and aware of the presence of a host of friends from the past looking over my shoulder.

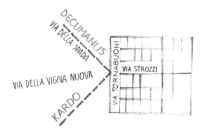

THE HISTORY OF FLORENCE

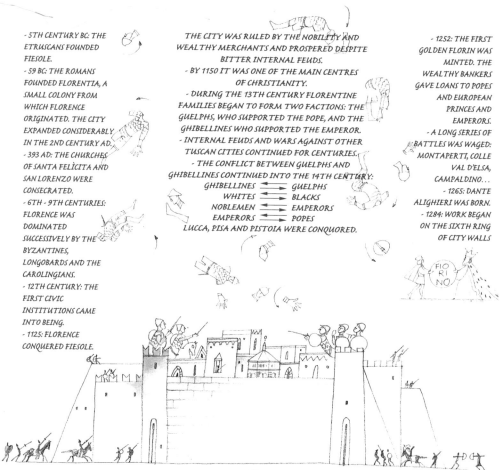

- 5TH CENTURY BC: THE ETRUSCANS FOUNDED FIESOLE.
- 59 BC: THE ROMANS FOUNDED FLORENTIA, A SMALL COLONY FROM WHICH FLORENCE ORIGINATED. THE CITY EXPANDED CONSIDERABLY IN THE 2ND CENTURY AD.
- 393 AD: THE CHURCHES OF SANTA FELÌCITA AND SAN LORENZO WERE CONSECRATED.
- 6TH - 9TH CENTURIES: FLORENCE WAS DOMINATED SUCCESSIVELY BY THE BYZANTINES, LONGOBARDS AND THE CAROLINGIANS.
- 12TH CENTURY: THE FIRST CIVIC INSTITUTIONS CAME INTO BEING.
- 1125: FLORENCE CONQUERED FIESOLE.

THE CITY WAS RULED BY THE NOBILITY AND WEALTHY MERCHANTS AND PROSPERED DESPITE BITTER INTERNAL FEUDS.
- BY 1150 IT WAS ONE OF THE MAIN CENTRES OF CHRISTIANITY.
- DURING THE 13TH CENTURY FLORENTINE FAMILIES BEGAN TO FORM TWO FACTIONS: THE GUELPHS, WHO SUPPORTED THE POPE, AND THE GHIBELLINES WHO SUPPORTED THE EMPEROR.
- INTERNAL FEUDS AND WARS AGAINST OTHER TUSCAN CITIES CONTINUED FOR CENTURIES.
- THE CONFLICT BETWEEN GUELPHS AND GHIBELLINES CONTINUED INTO THE 14TH CENTURY:

GHIBELLINES ⇄ GUELPHS
WHITES ⇄ BLACKS
NOBLEMEN ⇄ EMPERORS
EMPERORS ⇄ POPES
LUCCA, PISA AND PISTOIA WERE CONQUORED.

- 1252: THE FIRST GOLDEN FLORIN WAS MINTED. THE WEALTHY BANKERS GAVE LOANS TO POPES AND EUROPEAN PRINCES AND EMPERORS.
- A LONG SERIES OF BATTLES WAS WAGED: MONTAPERTI, COLLE VAL D'ELSA, CAMPALDINO...
- 1265: DANTE ALIGHIERI WAS BORN.
- 1284: WORK BEGAN ON THE SIXTH RING OF CITY WALLS

- IN THE LATE 13TH CENTURY NUMEROUS PUBLIC WORKS WERE UNDERTAKEN. THE SCULPTOR AND ARCHITECT, ARNOLFO DI CAMBIO, A MEMBER OF THE CIVIC COUNCIL, ENTIRELY REDESIGNED THE URBAN STRUCTURE AND INITIATED THE BUILDING OF CIVIL AND RELIGIOUS MONUMENTS. THERE WERE IMPORTANT DEVELOPMENTS IN PAINTING AND SCULPTURE: FLORENTINE ROMANESQUE BECAME POPULAR IN OTHER CITIES.

- THE MERCHANTS, GROUPED INTO TWENTY-ONE GUILDS, WERE RESPONSIBLE FOR THIS GROWTH AND DEVELOPMENT. THE SEVEN LARGEST GUILDS, BY FAR THE MOST IMPORTANT, BUILT CHURCHES, COMMISSIONED STATUES AND ALTAR PANELS... THE MOST POWERFUL WERE THE WOOL GUILD AND THE CALIMALA (CLOTH IMPORTERS).

- THE CITY WAS NOW DIVIDED BETWEEN THE BOURGEOISIE SUPPORTERS OF THE MEDICI, AND THE NOBILITY, WHO UPHELD THE ALBIZZI FAMILY. IN THE 14TH CENTURY THE CITY HAD 100,000 INHABITANTS: 10,000 CHILDREN KNEW HOW TO READ, MANY OF THEM STUDIED MATHEMATICS AND 500 STUDIED GRAMMAR AND LOGIC. THE VERNACULAR BEGAN TO REPLACE LATIN AS THE LANGUAGE OF LITERATURE: 'FLORENTINE' WAS BECOMING THE MODEL FOR A STANDARD ITALIAN LANGUAGE. IN FLORENCE THERE WERE 60 DOCTORS, 600 LAWYERS AND 80 BANKS. THE CITY WAS AWASH IN FLORINS, BUT DANTE DESCRIBED IT AS:

"... the wicked flower that turns the shepherds into ravening wolves and breaks the folds and lets the lambs run wild."

IN 1348 THE TERRIBLE 'BLACK DEATH' STRUCK FLORENCE. TWO PEOPLE IN EVERY THREE DIED. GIOVANNI BOCCACCIO'S 'DECAMERON' WAS SET IN THIS TRAGIC PERIOD.

- AROUND THE YEAR ONE THOUSAND THE BAPTISTERY, SAN MINIATO AND SANTA REPARATA, FLORENCE'S FIRST CATHEDRAL, WERE BUILT.
- FROM 1200 TO 1400 THE CITY'S OTHER MAIN CHURCHES WERE BUILT: SANTA MARIA DEL FIORE (THE NEW CATHEDRAL) SANTA CROCE SANTA MARIA NOVELLA SANTISSIMA ANNUNZIATA SANTO SPIRITO SANTA MARIA DEL CARMINE SANTA TRÌNITA THE BADIA FIORENTINA (ABBEY) THE BADIA FIESOLANA (ABBEY).
- IN THE 13TH CENTURY THE MAIN BRIDGES WERE BUILT IN WOOD.
- IN THE 15TH CENTURY MAGNIFICENT FRESCO CYCLES WERE PAINTED.

IN THE EARLY 14TH CENTURY CIVIL AND RELIGIOUS ARCHITECTURE ENJOYED A PERIOD OF RAPID DEVELOPMENT. NOT ONLY WAS GIOTTO'S BELL TOWER BUILT BUT THE SIGNORIA PALACE, THE LOGGIA DEL BIGALLO, THE BARGELLO (MAGISTRATE'S COURT AND PRISON) ORSANMICHELE, AS WELL AS MANY PRIVATE RESIDENCES: PALAZZO SPINI-FERONI, PALAZZO MOZZI, PALAZZO DAVANZATI... THE ANCIENT TOWER-HOUSES, VERITABLE URBAN FORTRESSES FROM WHENCE THE MOST POWERFUL FAMILIES WAGED WAR AGAINST EACH OTHER, WERE 'TRUNCATED' IN ORDER TO REDUCE THEIR HEIGHT.

CIMABUE AND HIS PUPIL, GIOTTO, BECAME FAMOUS. OTHER ARTISTS MADE NUMEROUS GOLD LEAF PANELS.

11

BETWEEN THE 14TH AND 15TH CENTURIES THE 'COMUNE', A UNIQUELY ITALIAN FORM OF A SMALL REPUBLIC, FREQUENTLY EVOLVED INTO A 'SIGNORIA'. A 'SIGNORIA' WAS THE DICTATORSHIP OF A RICH AND INFLUENTIAL PERSON WHOM THE BOURGEOISIE SUPPORTED AGAINST THE TRADITIONAL NOBILITY OF THE CITY. SOON THE POWER OF THIS INDIVIDUAL BECAME HEREDITARY AND THE FAMILY REPRESENTED AND CONSOLIDATED THEIR POSITION BY UNDERTAKING IMPORTANT PUBLIC WORKS WHICH STIMULATED PEOPLE'S IMAGINATION AND GAINED THEM POPULARITY. THUS NEW PUBLIC AND PRIVATE BUILDINGS APPEARED; SOMETIMES ENTIRE AREAS OF THE CITY WERE SWEPT AWAY TO MAKE PLACE FOR PRIVATE PALACES STANDING ON LARGE SQUARES. THESE CHANGES, HOWEVER, DID NOT GREATLY ALTER THE ANCIENT URBAN STRUCTURE AND MANY TWISTING MEDIEVAL ALLEYWAYS SURVIVED.

IN FLORENCE THE MEDICI ENCOURAGED THE STUDY OF ANTIQUITIES AND CLASSICAL LITERATURE AND SOME OF THE GREATEST POETS AND ARTISTS OF THE DAY BELONGED TO THEIR CULTURAL CIRCLE. AN INNOVATIVE PROCESS, LATER DEFINED AS THE RENAISSANCE, HAD BEGUN AND, IN VARIOUS GUISES, WAS TO CONTINUE THROUGHOUT THE 16TH CENTURY, GRADUALLY SPREADING INTO ALL EUROPEAN COUNTRIES. ARCHITECTURE, MUSIC, THEATRE, LITERATURE AND THE FIGURATIVE ARTS ALL FLOURISHED.

CLASSICAL ELEMENTS WERE REINTRODUCED USING NEW PROPORTIONS.

IRREGULAR AND UNPLANNED IN THE MIDDLE AGES, THE FAÇADE OF A BUILDING HAD NOW TO CONFORM TO THE CRITERIA OF HARMONY, SYMMETRY AND PROPORTION. THE STONEWORK WAS RUSTICATED USING LARGE, ROUGHLY HEWN CONVEX BLOCKS KNOWN AS ASHLARS.

RENAISSANCE

- POWER AND CRUELTY
- POVERTY AND SPLENDOUR
- POETRY AND HATRED
- REFINEMENTS AND ATROCITIES
- BLOOD AND MUSIC
- GLORY AND HORROR
- WAR AND LITERATURE
- ARTISTS AND MAGICIANS
- BEAUTY AND DESTRUCTION
- FESTIVALS AND INJUSTICE

1472. BENEDETTO DEI WROTE IN HIS 'HISTORY OF FLORENCE': "Beautiful Florence, it has twenty-three palaces, fifty squares and there are churches and houses around every square". THE MOST IMPORTANT FAMILIES HAVE THEIR OWN PALACE:
GONDI
GUADAGNI
GRIFONI
MARTELLI
PAZZI-QUARATESI
FRESCOBALDI
RUCELLAI
STROZZI
ANTINORI...

THE MEDICI FAMILY, ORIGINALLY FROM THE MUGELLO, BECAME WEALTHY THROUGH THE FINANCIAL DEALINGS OF GIOVANNI DI BICCI, FATHER OF COSIMO THE ELDER AND GREAT-GRANDFATHER OF LORENZO IL MAGNIFICO. THEY GAINED POLITICAL POWER DURING THE 15TH CENTURY, LATER BECOMING A FAMILY OF PRINCES, INCLUDING MILITARY COMMANDERS, GRAND DUKES, PRINCES AND EVEN TWO POPES AND TWO QUEENS OF FRANCE... PALAZZO MEDICI WAS BUILT IN VIA LARGA, AND PALAZZO DELLA SIGNORIA WAS TRANSFORMED INTO A MAGNIFICENT RESIDENCE FOR THE FAMILY; IT BECAME KNOW AS 'VECCHIO' (OLD) IN THE 16TH CENTURY WHEN THE GRAND DUKES MOVED TO PALAZZO PITTI. THE MEDICI GAVE THE CITY PORTICOS, LIBRARIES, THEATRES AND ACADEMIES.

SEVERAL STREETS BECOME PRESTIGIOUS:
MAGGIO (MAGGIORE - GREATER)
TORNABUONI
LARGA (NOW VIA CAVOUR)
DE' SERVI.

de Medici

MAN AND NATURE ARE
REDISCOVERED AND
REPRESENTED USING
THE RULES OF
PERSPECTIVE.

- PORTRAITS
- LANDSCAPES
- MUSIC
- DANCE
- POETRY
- ELOQUENCE
- ALCHEMY
- PHILOSOPHICAL
STUDIES...

AS AN ADJUNCT OF POWER,
THE ARTIST IS HELD IN
GREAT RESPECT:
- DONATELLO
- GHIBERTI
- BRUNELLESCHI
- MASACCIO
- PIERO DELLA FRANCESCA
- LEON BATTISTA ALBERTI
- BOTTICELLI
- GHIRLANDAIO
- LEONARDO
- MICHELANGELO
- RAPHAEL...

IN THE 16TH CENTURY, AS THE STATE OF FLORENCE GREW TO THE SIZE OF A
REGION, THE BOOK OF ETIQUETTE WRITTEN BY CARDINAL DELLA CASA
BECAME THE MODEL FOR ALL OF EUROPE.

1569: THE POPE MADE COSIMO I GRAND DUKE OF TUSCANY.

IN THE 17TH CENTURY FLORENCE BECAME THE EUROPEAN
CENTRE OF A NEW EXPERIMENTAL FORM OF SCIENCE.
GALILEO GALILEI WAS ITS PRINCIPAL EXPONENT.

1737: WITH THE DEATH OF GIANGASTONE DE' MEDICI THE GRAND DUCHY
PASSED TO THE HAPSBURG-LORRAINE EMPERORS WHO INTRODUCED
FAR-REACHING SOCIAL REFORMS. MANY RELIGIOUS ORDERS
WERE SUPPRESSED AND THE DEATH PENALTY WAS ABOLISHED.
THE 'CASCINE' BECAME A PUBLIC PARK.
1749: THE TRADITIONAL FLORENTINE CALENDAR WAS ABOLISHED
AND THE PRESENT ONE INTRODUCED.
1764 AND 1839: TWO RONDEAU WERE ADDED TO PALAZZO PITTI. SOME AREAS
OF THE CITY TOOK ON A SPECTACULAR APPEARANCE AND THE FIRST
PICTURESQUE VIEWS CAME INTO EXISTENCE.
GRAND DUKE PIETRO LEOPOLDO IMPROVED THE STANDARD OF LIFE IN THE CITY
AND MODERNIZED THE ROAD SYSTEM.

DURING NAPOLEON'S OCCUPATION OF THE GRAND DUCHY, HE ENTRUSTS
THE GOVERNMENT OF TUSCANY TO HIS SISTER, ELISA BACIOCCHI.
THE SUPPRESSION OF RELIGIOUS ORDERS CONTINUES WITH IMPORTANT CONSEQUENCES FOR THE URBAN
ARCHITECTURE: ENTIRE MEDIEVAL AREAS DISAPPEAR, STREETS AND SQUARES BECOME LARGER,
RESIDENTIAL AREAS COME IN TO BEING.
INTELLECTUALS INCLUDE THE CITY IN THEIR GRAND TOUR.

1865-1870: FLORENCE BECOMES THE CAPITAL OF ITALY. THE URBAN EXPANSION CONTINUES:
AVENUES ARE MADE AND SCENIC AREAS ARE CREATED.
THE FLOOD OF 1966 SERIOUSLY DAMAGED THE CITY'S ARTISTIC HERITAGE
AND MUCH REBUILDING AND RESTORATION WAS UNDERTAKEN.
UNESCO HAS DECLARED FLORENCE OF 'OUTSTANDING UNIVERSAL VALUE'.
THE MAGGIO MUSICALE CONCERT AND OPERA SEASON AND THE TRADE FAIRS ENLIVEN THE LIFE OF THE CITY.
MILLIONS OF VISITORS COME TO ADMIRE THE CITY EVERY YEAR.

THE ARNO

"...and they held parties on the Arno, usually between the Santa Trinita and the Carraia bridges..."
A. Lapini,
'A Florentine Diary',
c. 1550.

Carp
pike
tench
ducks
house-martins
seagulls
coypu
but also jewels
and fishermen
canoes and suntans
regattas
and sparkling glints.

Detail from the Uffizi Gallery by Francesco Botticini.

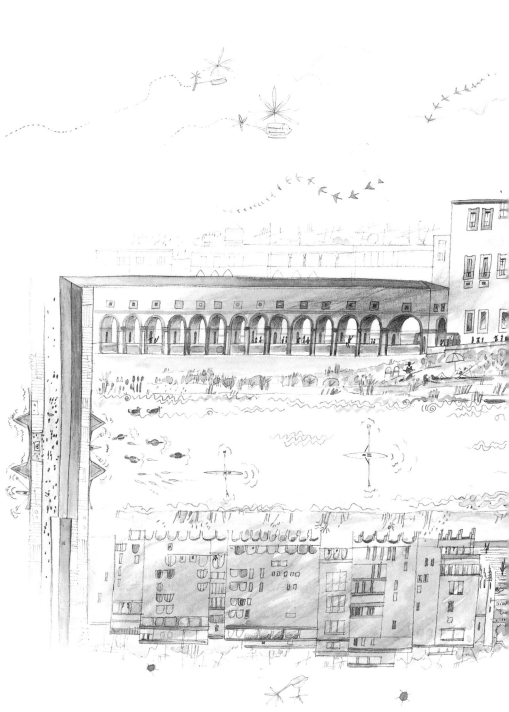

THE VASARI CORRIDOR, UFFIZI GALLERY, SCIENCE MUSEUM.
"… along the banks where smiling Arno sweeps…" Lord Byron, c. 1821.

PALAZZO CAPPONI and more palaces, cypress trees, gardens.

FLORENTINE ROMANESQUE

SANTA MARIA DEL FIORE:
THE CATHEDRAL
BAPTISTERY
SAN SALVATORE AL VESCOVO
SANTA MARIA NOVELLA
SANTO STEFANO AL PONTE

"1294. The people of Florence ordered that the
Church should be renewed... it was to be made
in marble... and it was to be named Santa
Maria del Fiore..."
A. Lapini, 'A Florentine Diary', c. 1550.

PIAZZA DUOMO should only be visited in the early morning

THE DOOR KNOWN AS THE BELL-TOWER DOOR

THE CATHEDRAL MUSEUM

pulleys, drills, wooden hoists, buckles,... tools that still show the immense effort involved and amaze and impress us.

"... Filippo alone said that it could be raised without a great deal of woodwork, without piers or earth, at far less expense than arches would entail, and very easily without any framework..."
G. Vasari, 'Lives of the Artists', 1550.

BRUNELLESCHI AND THE DOME

· inventiveness
· imagination
· tension
· strength
· jealousy
· resentment
· escape
· regrets
· desperation
· effort
· glory
· and...
one hundred florins a year.

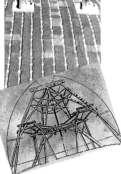

The bricks seen on the inside are arranged in herring-bone fashion.

"Well, now what are we going to do, Master Filippo?"

The mask in the Cathedral Museum

"5th April 1492: At about 3 at night (11 pm.) the lantern of the dome of Santa Maria del Fiore was struck by a thunderbolt and it was split almost in half that is, one of the marble niches and many other pieces of marble were taken off…"

L. Landucci, 'A Florentine Diary', c. 1492.

"… every day it is struck by lightning." G. Vasari, 'Lives of the Artists', 1550.

a fourteenth-century marble holy water stoop, rich with simbolic ornamentation.

• THE SACRISTY IS DECORATED WITH WOOD INLAY, SCULPTED ANGELS, STATUES AND MARBLE SCULPTURES.

• PAINTED ALTAR PANELS.

• STAINED GLASS.

• IT TOOK FIFTEEN YEARS TO RESTORE THE FRESCOES IN THE DOME.

• THE PLAN IS IN THE FORM OF A LATIN CROSS.

• THE 14TH CENTURY FLOOR IS A RAINBOW OF COLOURED MARBLE.

• BRONZE DOORS.

• FRESCOES.

• THE SCULPTED BALUSTER.

· A VAST RANGE OF TONES FROM GREY TO OCHRE.
· CANDLES, LIGHTS, MUSIC, ECHOES, WHISPERS.

STAINED GLASS WINDOWS
MADE IN THE 14TH AND
15TH CENTURIES; SOME
WERE DESIGNED BY
DONATELLO, GHIBERTI,
PAOLO UCCELLO.

A PROFUSION OF
VIVID COLOURS.

very beautiful
when the sun shines through.

"you can get glass in all colours . . ."
C. Cennini, 'The Craftsman's Handbook', c. 1395.
"great mastery is needed in glass mosaic to arrange the pieces so harmoniously that it appears a genuine and beautiful picture."
G. Vasari, 'On Technique', from 'Lives of the Artists', 1550.

EAST DOOR:
MICHELANGELO CALLED IT THE 'DOOR OF PARADISE'.

M.CCV

THE BAPTISTERY OF SAN GIOVANNI

"The people of Florence had black and white marble and columns from many places brought by sea and then by the Arno… with great diligence they made it most beautiful and noble with eight sides."
G. Villani, 'Nuova Cronica', 1350.

"Then work began on the most beautiful bronze doors, wonderfully worked and then polished and gilded."
M. Villani, 'Nuova Cronica', 1360.

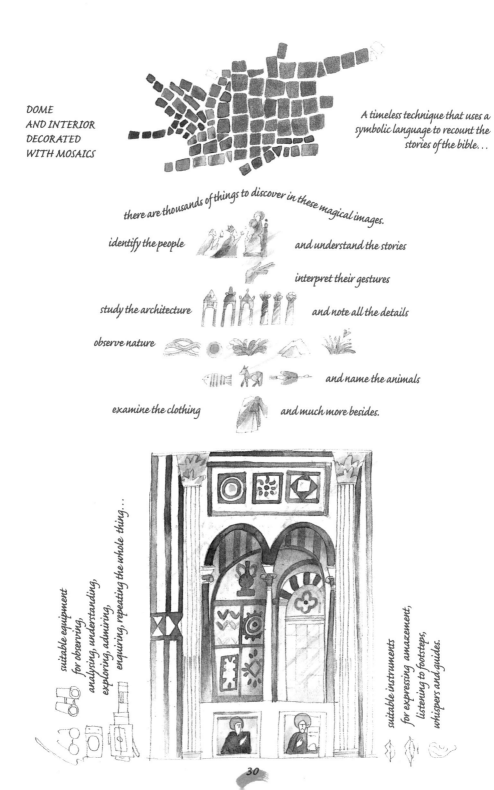

DOME
AND INTERIOR
DECORATED
WITH MOSAICS

A timeless technique that uses a symbolic language to recount the stories of the bible...

there are thousands of things to discover in these magical images.

identify the people

and understand the stories

interpret their gestures

study the architecture

and note all the details

observe nature

and name the animals

examine the clothing

and much more besides.

suitable equipment for observing, analysing, understanding, exploring, admiring, enquiring, repeating the whole thing...

suitable instruments for expressing amazement, listening to footsteps, whispers and guides.

ANGELS, ARCHANGELS, PROPHETS, PATRIARCHS, RELIGIOUS STORIES.
A MYRIAD OF FIGURES COVERS THE EIGHT SEGMENTS
and your eyes never tire of looking.

MOSAIC AND ALL THE COLOURS OF THE TESSERAE

The marquis Emilio Pucci, a famous
Florentine fashion designer, was often
inspired by the decorations
of the Baptistery.

DANTE OFTEN REFERRED
TO THE BAPTISTERY
AND SOMETIMES EVEN HAD FUN
WEARING EMILIO PUCCI'S GLASSES.
THE MARBLE ZODIAC
SET INTO THE PAVEMENT
DATES FROM 1209.
IN THE CENTRE IS AN IMAGE OF THE SUN,
AROUND IT A TEXT IN LATIN WHICH CAN BE
READ FROM BOTH LEFT AND RIGHT.
"EN GIRO TORTE SOL CICLOS ET ROTOR IGNE"

"… my lovely San Giovanni,…"

Dante Alighieri, 'The Divine Comedy',

c. 1307-21.

· 24 JUNE: THE FEAST OF SAN GIOVANNI.
EVERY YEAR ON THIS DAY A PARADE OF FIVE HUNDRED AND THIRTY FLORENTINES
IN 16TH-CENTURY COSTUME IS HELD.
THE PROCESSION PRECEDES A FOOTBALL MATCH IN HISTORIC COSTUME WHICH COMMEMORATES
THE GAME PLAYED IN 1530 WHILE THE ARMY OF CHARLES V BOMBED THE CITY.

standard bearers, banners, flags, halberds, swords...

captain of the artillery

superintendent

sargent of the civic guard and chief and executive of the rural guard

Florentine flag-bearer and herald of the signoria

bowsmen and infantry of the state.

captain of the guilds, major general of the army, the team, magistrate of the five custodians of the Florentine rural area proconsul of the guilds, tribune of goods and produce, colonels and captains of the cavalry.

37

THE CLOISTERS

THE COLOURS
OF THE CLOISTERS IN
THE CHOISTRO VERDE
(GREEN CLOISTER).

A DETAIL OF
THE MAIN CHAPEL.

SANTA MARIA NOVELLA
THE CLOISTERS, THE SPANISH CHAPEL.

SAN LORENZO
THE CLOISTER
THE LAURENTIAN LIBRARY
AND THE DAILY MARKET.

Michelangelo's windows.

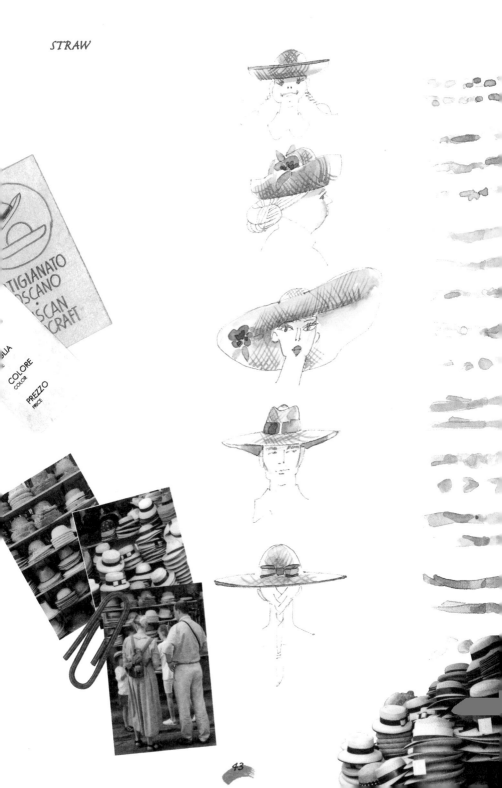

STRAW

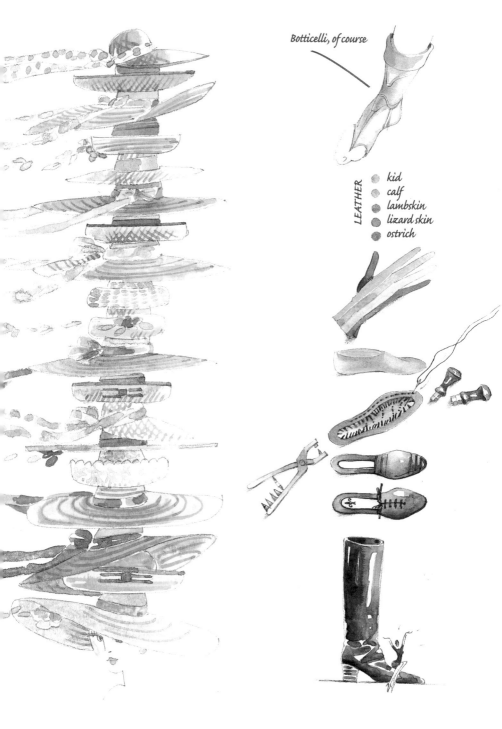

Botticelli, of course

LEATHER
- kid
- calf
- lambskin
- lizard skin
- ostrich

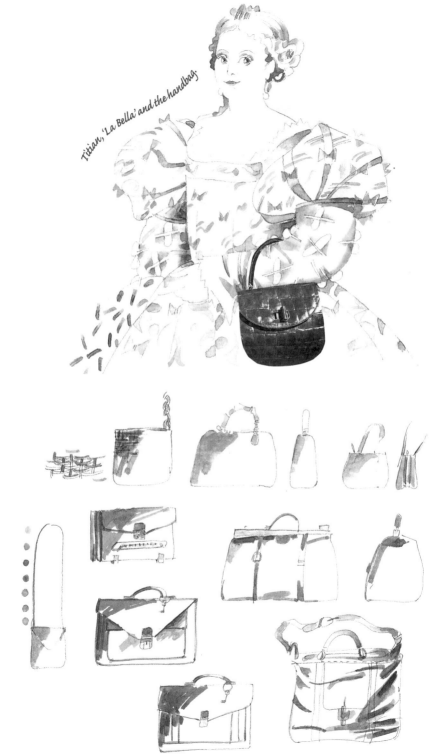

Titian, 'La Bella' and the handbag.

COLOURED LEATHER

"Below the window should run a parapet of stone ... on which
the doves can alight or take flight on leaving."
L. B. Alberti, 'De re Ædificatoria', 1452.

and in Via del Proconsolo, the bus just trots along

BARGELLO

LOGGIA

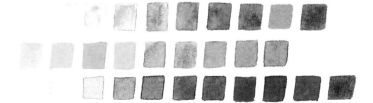

THE BARDINI MUSEUM
Giovanni della Robbia
would like to have more visitors
but for now there's only
the two of us

THE BARGELLO
PAINTINGS
FURNITURE
WEAPONS
COINS
SCULPTURES

terracottas by the Della Robbia and all their lovely colours.

"In Florence … the Grand Duke goes everywhere on horseback…"
E. Lear, "Letters", 1833.

PERSEUS: THE NEPTUNE FOUNTAIN, CARRIAGES… UNUSUAL SIGHTS IN PIAZZA DELLA SIGNORIA.

PIAZZA DELLA SIGNORIA AND PALAZZO VECCHIO
"1298. In this year the building of the grand and beautiful Palazzo de' Priori was begun..."
A. Lapini, 'A Florentine Diary', c.1550.

LIUTAIO

In the shadow of Palazzo Vecchio traditional tripe sandwiches are sold and rare musical instruments are made.

PALAZZO VECCHIO: THE FIRST COURTYARD.

VEROCCHIO'S 'PUTTO WITH A DOLPHIN' SEEN FROM FOUR SIDES.

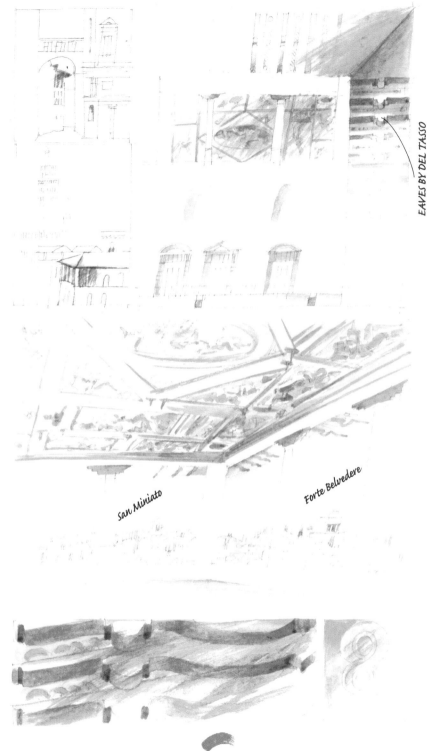

PALAZZO VECCHIO: THE SATURN TERRACE

EAVES BY DEL TASSO

San Miniato

Forte Belvedere

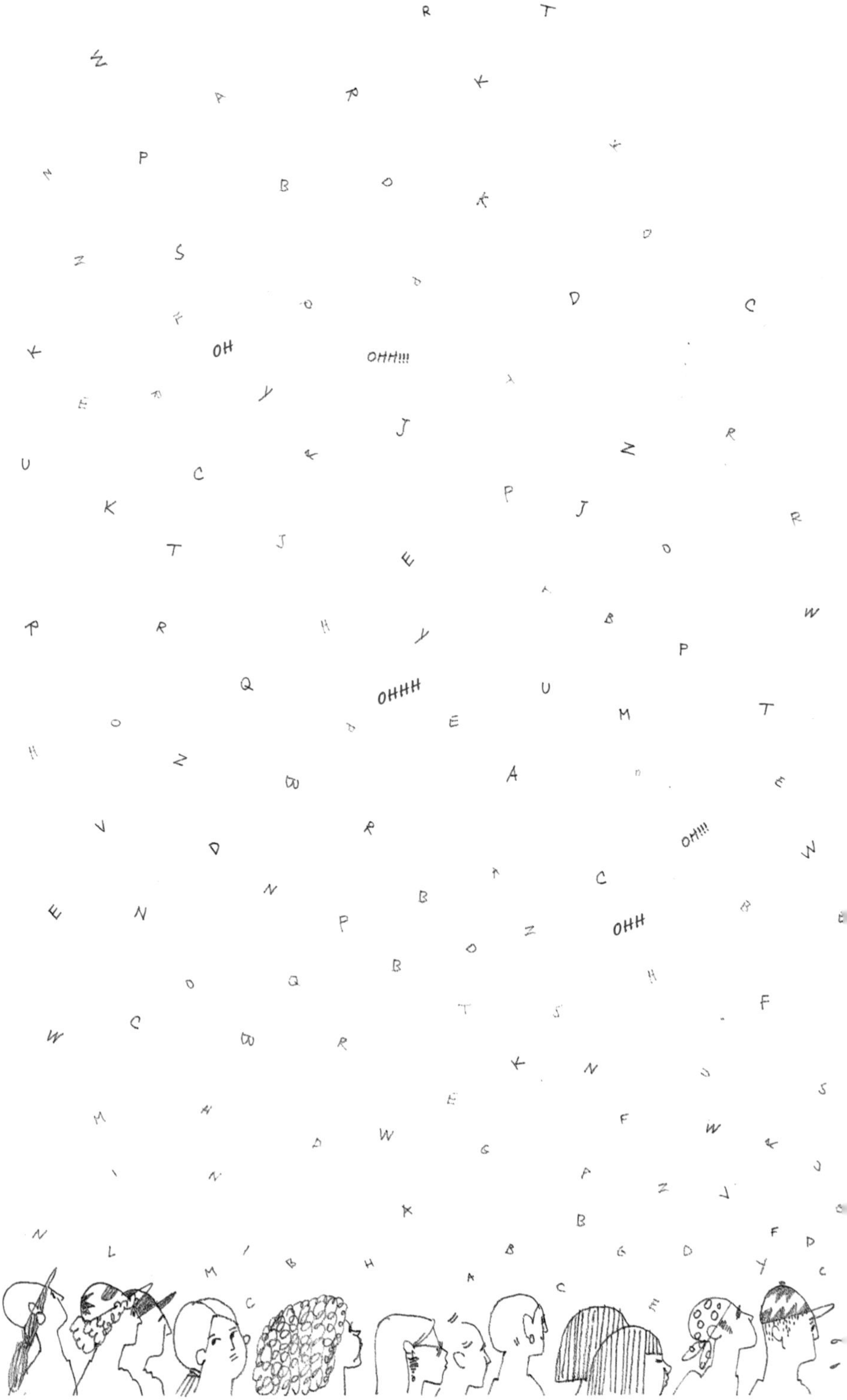
OH
OHH!!!
OHHH
OH!!!
OHH

SIGNS

OHH!!!

PEOPLE GOING TO AND FRO BETWEEN
PIAZZA DUOMO AND PIAZZA SIGNORIA

FLORENTINES GOING TOWARDS PIAZZA DUOMO
FLORENTINES GOING TOWARDS PIAZZA SIGNORIA
ADULTS AND YOUNGSTERS GOING TOWARDS PIAZZA DUOMO
ADULTS AND YOUNGSTERS GOING TOWARDS PIAZZA SIGNORIA
STUDENTS
SOLDIERS LOOKING FOR GIRLS
GIRLS WAITING FOR SOLDIERS

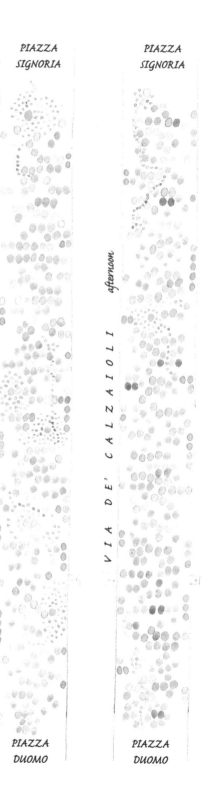

PIAZZA
SIGNORIA

PIAZZA
SIGNORIA

morning

afternoon

VIA DE' CALZAIOLI

VIA DE' CALZAIOLI

PIAZZA
DUOMO

PIAZZA
DUOMO

VIA DE' CALZAIOLI
ALWAYS AN IMPORTANT STREET,
"pulchra ampla et recta",
in 1350 it was already paved.

GIORGIO VASARI PIT. ET
ARCHITET. ARETINO

POSTE ITALIANE L.90
1266 GIOTTO 1337

VFIZII

PIAZZA DEL
GRAN DVCA

UFFIZI

SERIE C

N° 772478

REPUBBLICA ITALIANA
MINISTERO PER I BENI CULTURALI E AMBIENTALI
UFFICIO CENTRALE PER I BENI AMBIENTALI
ARCHITETTONICI ARCHEOLOGICI ARTISTICI E STORICI

BIGLIETTO D'INGRESSO
LIRE 10.000

GALLERIA degli UFFIZI

GIORGIO VASARI 1511-1574

ITALIA L.90

GIUNTI S.P.A.
GRUPPO EDITOR.
GALLERIA UFFIZI
P.LE UFFIZI FI
P.I.0314600481
CARTOLINE

LIBRI   5.500
             20.000
TOTALE   25.500
CONTANTE
14-04-99   608
AZ7BB 6620789

61

on sale in the best shops
'Uffizi' series 'The Birth of Venus' by Botticelli
printed fabric - 1m x 1.5 m
100% cotton
made in Italy.

in your own home!

THE UFFIZI GALLERY and some visitors

ROOMS IN THE GALLERY
THE 13TH CENTURY
THE SIENESE 14TH CENTURY
THE FLORENTINE 14TH CENTURY
INTERNATIONAL GOTHIC.

gold
gold
gold
and the brightest
colours

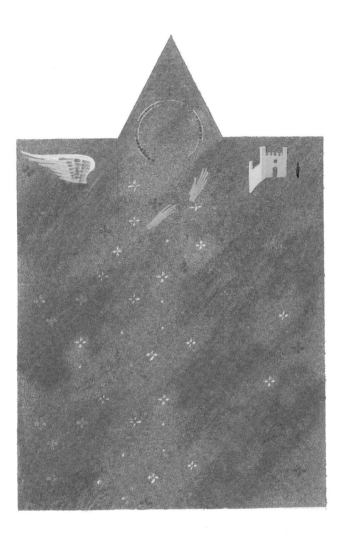

"It was truly a most beautiful secret and an ingenious invention that discovery of the method of beating gold into such thin leaves... that the wood and other material hidden beneath it should appear a mass of gold."
G. Vasari, 'On Technique', from 'Lives of the Artists', 1550.

VIRGIN AND CHILD
ANGELS
SAINTS
CLIFFS
CASTLES

and thousands of little tales

Duccio

Giotto

Cimabue

Frames

IOhARELIO

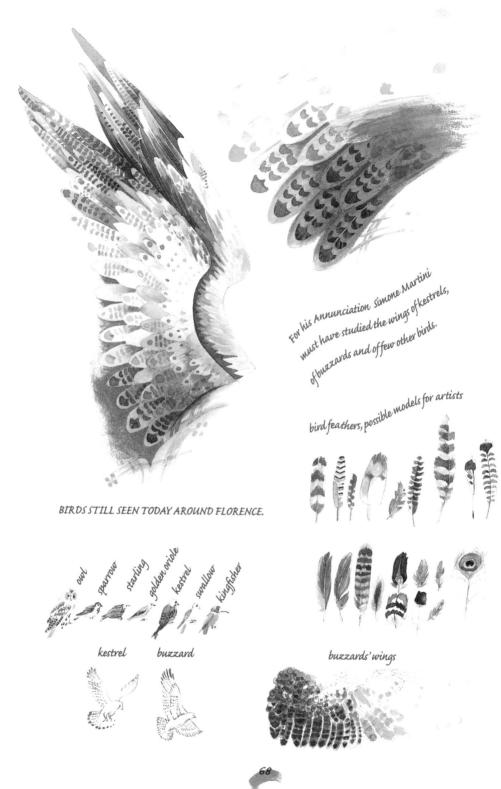

For his Annunciation Simone Martini must have studied the wings of kestrels, of buzzards and of few other birds.

bird feathers, possible models for artists

BIRDS STILL SEEN TODAY AROUND FLORENCE.

owl   sparrow   starling   golden oriole   kestrel   swallow   kingfisher

kestrel   buzzard

buzzards' wings

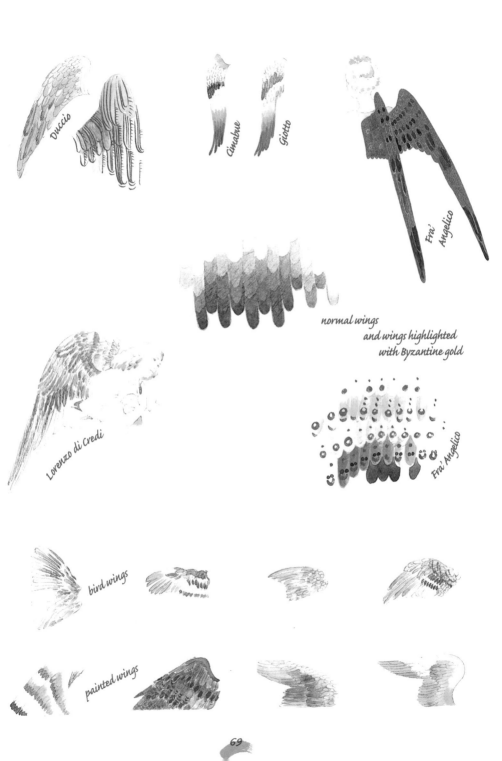

Duccio

Cimabue

Giotto

Fra' Angelico

normal wings
and wings highlighted
with Byzantine gold

Lorenzo di Credi

Fra' Angelico

bird wings

painted wings

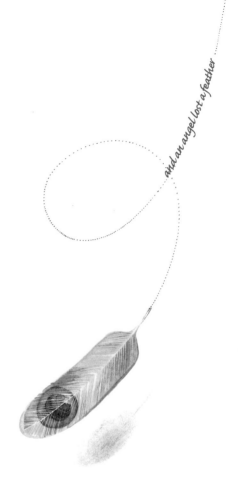

...and an angel lost a feather

71

ANGELS
1200-1300

1400-1500

1600

TOOLS OF THE TRADE

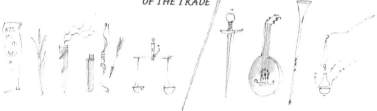

ENEMIES (BUT NOT ALL THE TIME)

Duccio

Giotto

Cimabue

THE UFFIZI GALLERY AT NIGHT.

OH!!!

THE BOTTICELLI ROOM
DOMENICO GHIRLANDAIO
HUGO VAN DER GOES

and some details

ANDY WARHOL IMAGINED
THE FACE OF BOTTICELLI'S
'VENUS' BLUE.
BUT SOME BOYS
IMAGINE HER LIKE THIS.

and one of the 'Three Graces' revisited.

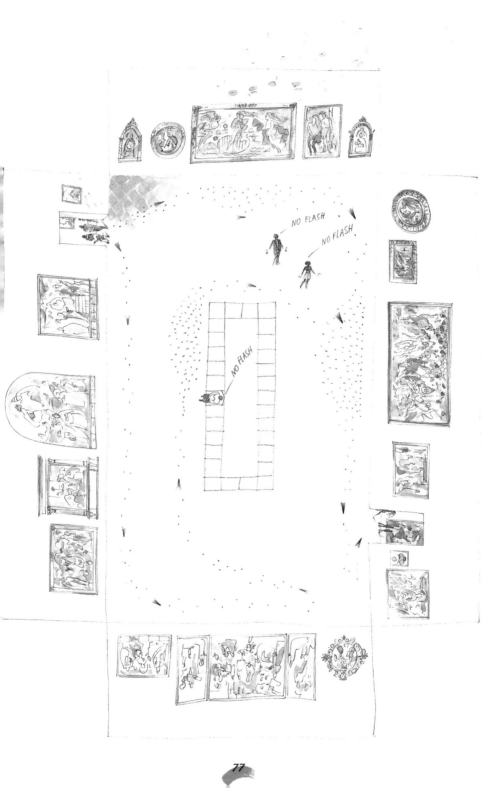

NO FLASH

NO FLASH

NO FLASH

77

The Botticelli Room: surrounded by admirers.

at 9.10 am   9.20   9.30

10.00 'Primavera' makes an excuse and leaves...

she rushes off to try on Ferragamo's brightly coloured sandals.

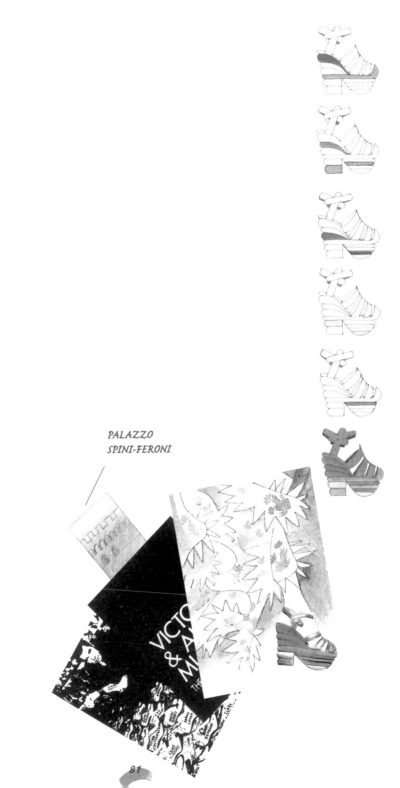

PALAZZO
SPINI-FERONI

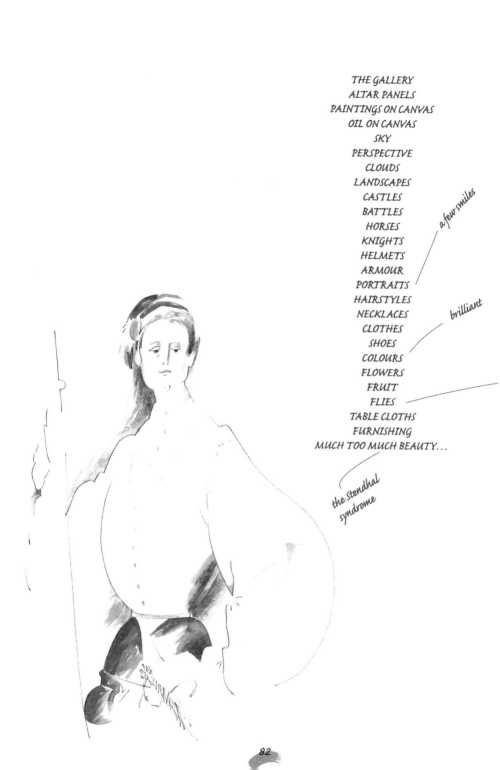

THE GALLERY
ALTAR PANELS
PAINTINGS ON CANVAS
OIL ON CANVAS
SKY
PERSPECTIVE
CLOUDS
LANDSCAPES
CASTLES
BATTLES
HORSES
KNIGHTS
HELMETS
ARMOUR
PORTRAITS
HAIRSTYLES
NECKLACES
CLOTHES
SHOES
COLOURS
FLOWERS
FRUIT
FLIES
TABLE CLOTHS
FURNISHING
MUCH TOO MUCH BEAUTY...

a few smiles

brilliant

the Stendhal syndrome

always to be found
n 17th-century
till life

Some visitors to the gallery stare puzzled at the new hair style of Battista Sforza.

"… take a large quantity
of well washed herbs …"
from a 14th century recipe book

FLORENTINE TRIPE

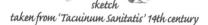

TUSCAN COOKING IS RUSTIC IN STYLE
AND MAKES USE OF THE BEST INGREDIENTS:
A LOT OF OLIVE OIL
THE FRESHEST VEGETABLES
AROMATIC HERBS
DELICIOUS MEAT
UNSALTED BREAD.

sketch
taken from 'Tacuinum Sanitatis' 14th century

"… beans: the best are reddish and whole…"

'Tacuinum Sanitatis'
14th century

"… They heat up the beans…
and they make virile seed"
Pietro Mattioli, 'Commentarii in sex…', 1565.

Tuscans were nicknamed
'bean-eaters'
for the great quantities
they eat.

"… roast meat
has more flavour
than stewed meat, beca…
it cooks in its own juices,
but a stew
in other juices…" from …
14th century recipe book

1533: ALESSANDRO DE' MEDICI
PRESENTED A BEAN PLANT TO
HIS SISTER CATHERINE ON
HER MARRIAGE TO THE
FUTURE KING HENRY II OF
FRANCE.
1600: MARIA DE' MEDICI
MARRIED HENRY IV OF
FRANCE.

"... to live well we need good and healthy food...
... the table should always have plentiful wine and bread..."
A. Pandolfini, 'Treatise on the Family', 1400.

Oil

Salt

Pepper

THE MOST FAMOUS DISH
IS THE TRADITIONAL 'BISTECCA ALLA FIORENTINA',
A STEAK FROM AN OX OF THE CHIANINA BREED,
COOKED ON THE GRILL AND THEN SEASONED
WITH OIL, SALT AND PEPPER;
ACCOMPANY
WITH UNSALTED BREAD, BEANS...

... and a glass of Chianti.

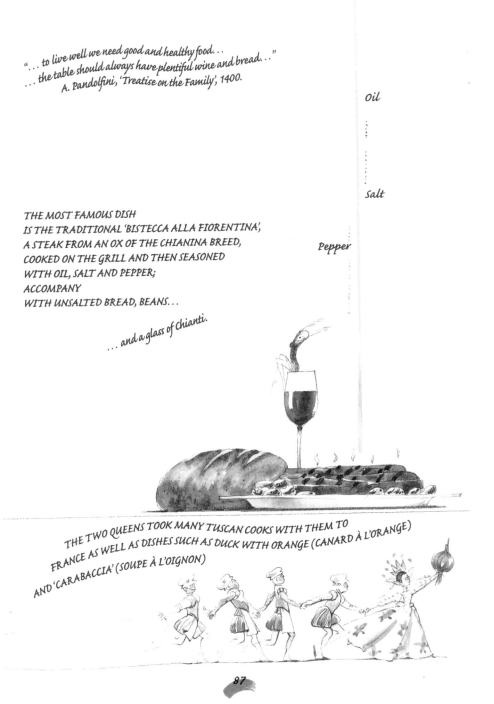

THE TWO QUEENS TOOK MANY TUSCAN COOKS WITH THEM TO
FRANCE AS WELL AS DISHES SUCH AS DUCK WITH ORANGE (CANARD À L'ORANGE)
AND 'CARABACCIA' (SOUPE À L'OIGNON)

TRADITIONAL FOOD

1   UNSALTED TUSCAN BREAD
2   EXTRAVIRGIN OLIVE OIL
3   CROSTINI
4   SLICED COLD MEATS
5   PANZANELLA (BREAD SALAD)
6   RIBOLLITA *just as good cold!*
    (BREAD AND VEGETABLE SOUP)
7   PAPPA AL POMODORO
    (BREAD AND TOMATO SOUP)
8   PASTA BOWS AND PEAS
9   RAVIOLI WITH BUTTER AND SAGE
10 BEAN SOUP
11 MIXED ROAST MEATS
12 FLORENTINE TRIPE
13 BEANS IN TOMATO SAUCE
14 ARTICHOKES
15 FLORENTINE ICE
16 SNAILS
17 FLORENTINE PEAS
18 FRIED COURGETTE FLOWERS
19 BEANS IN A JAR
20 FLAVOURED RICOTTA
21 PECORINO CHEESE AND PEARS
22 MOUNTAINS OF ICE CREAM
23 VARIATIONS ON ICE CREAM
24 ZUCCOTTO
25 TORTA DELLA NONNA
    (GRANNY'S CAKE)
26 ARNO SWEETIES
27 PARADISE CAKE
28 VIN SANTO AND
    ALMOND BISCUITS

1

6

15

16

17

22

23

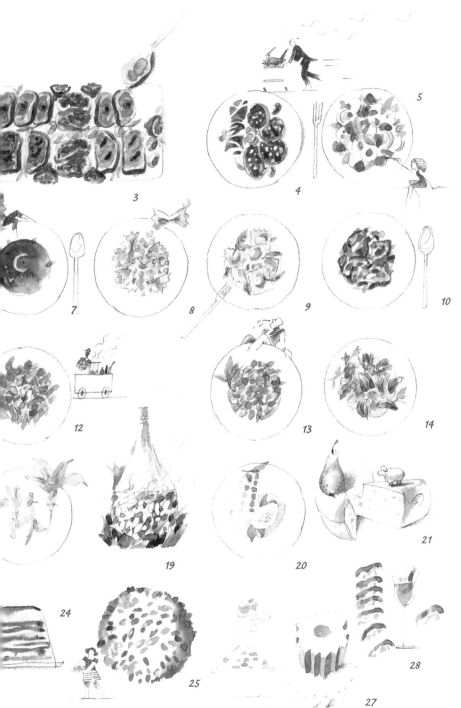

3

4

5

7

8

9

10

12

13

14

19

20

21

24

25

26

27

28

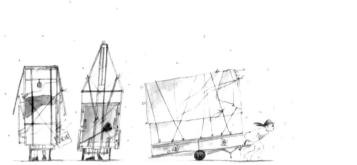

AT 6.30 PM

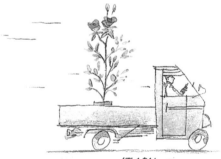

AT 4 PM

AT 7 AM

PALAZZO DAVANZATI

COURTYARD
THE GREAT HALL
SOME DETAILS

and the floors all smell of wax

AMORE MI PORTA ALLEGREZZA

AMORE MI PORTA ALLEGREZZA

9, 26 aprile
Giuliano De Me

"...the kitchen should be... merry and airy... with high and wide fireplaces..." B. Scappi, 'Opera', 1580.

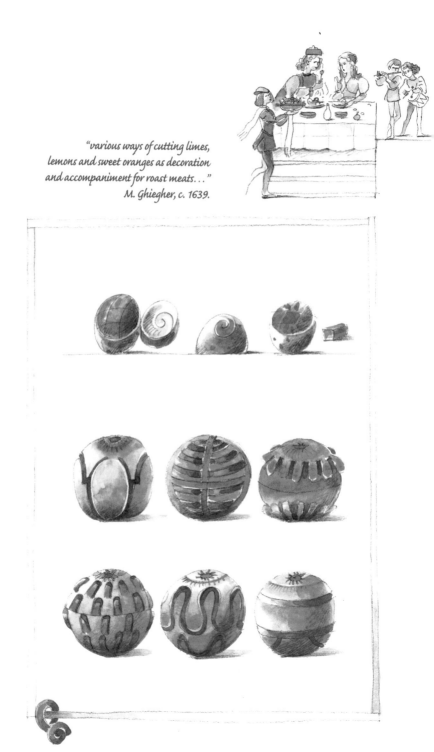

"various ways of cutting limes, lemons and sweet oranges as decoration and accompaniment for roast meats..."
M. Ghiegher, c. 1639.

vermicelli
maccheroni
lasagna
pike
turbot
crayfish
sardines

pheasant
partridge
veal
deer
leeks
brocoli
asparagus
cress
endive

but
sometimes
poison got
into the
dishes

"… he washed his hands in perfumed water and immediately and speedily the diligent stewards brought to the table … artichokes, cooked and uncooked… tender peas in their pod…" V. Cervio, 'Il Trinciante', 1580.

· THE ARCHAEOLOGICAL
  MUSEUM

· OPIFICIO
  DELLE
  PIETRE
  DURE

· PITTI

THE PAZZI CHAPEL and the swallows

PIAZZALE MICHELANGELO
no longer do Goethe, Byron, .Mc Carthy admire the view,
but Mario Rossi, John Smith, Pierre Daniel, Beate Meier.

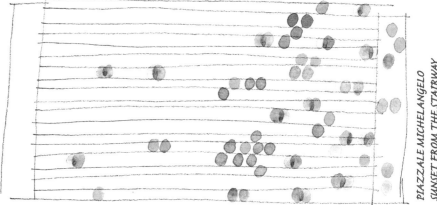

COUPLES

BABIES

PEOPLE ON THEIR OWN

GIRLS ALONE

SOLDIERS

GIRLS PLAYING THE GUITAR

DECEMBER 6 - 16 p.m.

AUGUST 17 - 20 p.m.

J F M A M J J A S O N D

OLTRARNO
PALAZZO PITTI
THE BOBOLI GARDENS
BARDINI MUSEUM
THE CARMINE CHURCH
SANTO SPIRITO
SAN FREDIANO IN CESTELLO
PIAZZALE MICHELANGELO
THE IRIS GARDEN
SAN MINIATO AL MONTE

NORD

O · E

S

GIARDINO DELL'IRIS A FIRENZE

Giardino o Piazza dell'Anfiteatro.
Viale in piaggia che dall'Anfiteatro sale al Nettuno.
Peschiera di Nettuno.
Viale ombroso che conduce al Casino sotto la Fortezza.
Palazzetto detto del Cavaliere.

Santo
Spirito

Eleonora di Toledo at Pitti palace

'Eleonora di Toledo
with Her Son Giovanni', c. 1545.
Agnolo Bronzino, Uffizi Gallery .

The 'Tribune', always very popular,
is an intimate setting but packed with works of art,
including the portrait of Eleonora.

velvet, brocade, bouclé, made in Florence, c. 1550.
The Bargello Museum, Carrand collection.

THE CLOTH
MADE IN FLORENCE
WAS ADMIRED
BY MANY EUROPEAN RULERS.
ELEONORA SUPERVISED
THE WORK, SOME OF WHICH
WAS CARRIED OUT AT
PALAZZO PITTI.
THE FABRIC OF THE DRESS
IN BRONZINO'S PORTRAIT
(RUFFLES AND CURLS OF GOLD IN
RELIEF ON A WHITE BACKGROUND)
WAS MOST PRECIOUS DUE TO THE
DIFFICULT PROCESSES INVOLVED.

White inset

Relief gold filigree

Velvet

Velvet

Velvet

"The duchess asked me
to make a girdle of gold;
with jewels and many
fine inventions..."
B. Cellini, 'The Life of Benvenuto Cellini'
c. 1558-66.

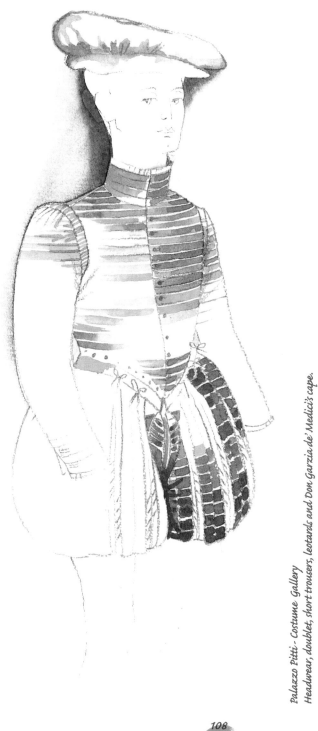

Palazzo Pitti - Costume Gallery
Headwear, doublet, short trousers, leotards and Don Garzia de' Medici's cape.

'FASHION AT THE COURT OF THE MEDICI'
IMAGINATIVELY INTERPRETED BY JANET ARNOLD.

BUONTALENTI'S FOUNTAIN IN PIAZZA FRESCOBALDI.

PALAZZO PITTI: THE FAÇADE LOOKING TOWARDS THE BOBOLI GARDENS.

Henry II of France:
"Well, Catherine, my dear
will have ten children, but I
just given the Castle of Chenon
to Diane of Poitiers".

Palazzo Pitti,
the Palatine Gallery:
the four walls of the Iliad room
and the (nocturnal) conversations
of the characters.

*'La Gravida'
by Raphael*

*'Maria de' Medici'
by Scipione Pulzone*

*Portrait of a Lady
by Ridolfo del Ghirlandaio*

I want to get out!

Maria de' Medici: "Pulzo
painted me here, but whe
the wife of Henry IV and qu
France, I will make Fran
the Younger court pain

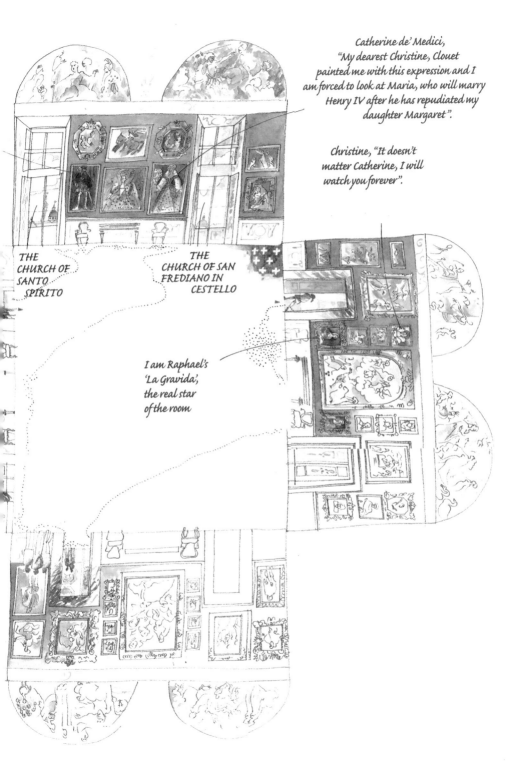

Catherine de' Medici, "My dearest Christine, Clouet painted me with this expression and I am forced to look at Maria, who will marry Henry IV after he has repudiated my daughter Margaret".

Christine, "It doesn't matter Catherine, I will watch you forever".

THE CHURCH OF SANTO SPIRITO

THE CHURCH OF SAN FREDIANO IN CESTELLO

I am Raphael's 'La Gravida', the real star of the room

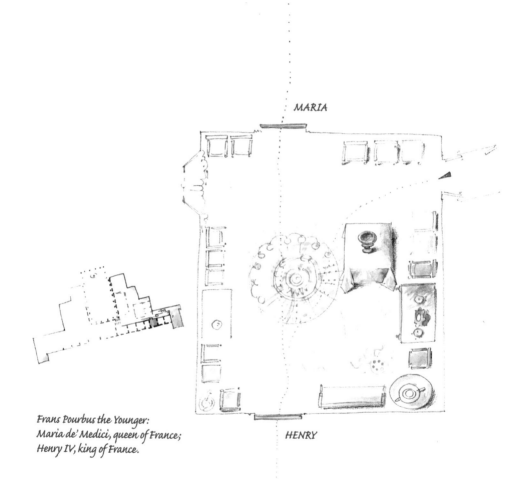

MARIA

HENRY

Frans Pourbus the Younger:
Maria de' Medici, queen of France;
Henry IV, king of France.

words, words, words.

THE BOBOLI GARDENS
"Of statues in the garden I do not disapprove . . . " L. B. Alberti, 'De re Ædificatoria', 1452.

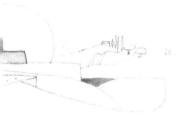

Bernardo Buontalenti,

*THE BEL VEDERE FORT: above the Fort
is an elegant little palace.*

THE CHURCH OF SANTO SPIRITO:
A MOST ORIGINAL IDEA BY MARIO MARIOTTI,
VARIOUS INTERPRETATIONS OF THE FAÇADE.

ETC·ETC·

THE CHURCH OF SANTO SPIRITO

MUSEO BARDINI

papier-mâché mannequins
and a detail of a hair style.

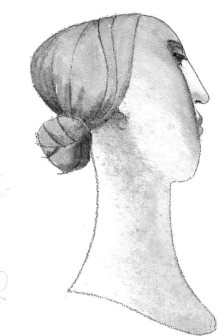

COLOURS AND PATINA
pale ochre
light fleshy pink
pinkish orange
off white
dull crimson
traces of black

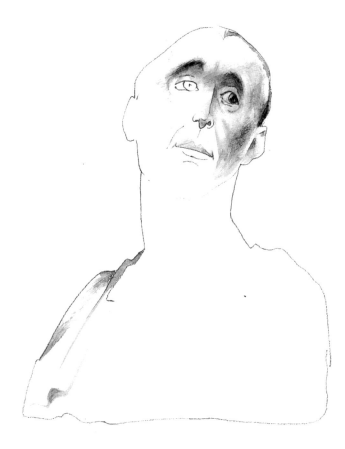

'Niccolo da Uzzano' coloured terracotta. By Donatello, Bargello Museum.

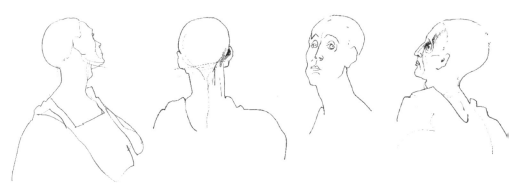

Florentine iris

THE IRIS,
OR LILY OF FLORENCE, IS
TRADITIONALLY GROWN
NEAR TO OLIVE TREES.
SINCE THE MIDDLE AGES,
IT HAS BEEN THE
SYMBOL OF FLORENCE.

May:
the festival of the iris is held
in Piazzale Michelangelo.

bearded iris
standard
stylus
beard
stamen
petal
ovate

crest
anther
stigma
filament

a skilful flagbearer brandishes the banner during a procession

GIOVANNI VILLANI WROTE:
"Where the city was built, flowers
and lilies grow"
G. Villani, 'Cronicle of Florence',
1350.

THE LILIES ARE
EVERYWHERE, AND ARE EVEN
USED TO DECORATE THE
WALLS OF SOME PALACES.
  SALA DEI GIGLI (THE LILY
  ROOM)
  IN PALAZZO VECCHIO;
  SALA DEI PAVONI
  (THE PEACOCK ROOM)
  IN PALAZZO DAVANZATI.

'Galeazzo Maria Sforza', 1471. By Piero del Pollaiolo, Uffizi Gallery.

THE CHURCH OF SAN MINIATO AT DUSK

VIEW OF THE INTERIOR OF THE CHURCH

SAN MINIATO

THE SURROUNDING COUNTRYSIDE

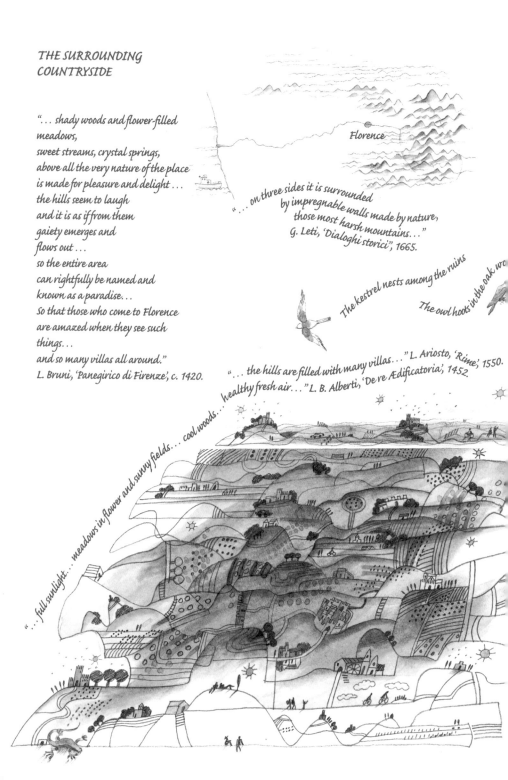

"… shady woods and flower-filled
meadows,
sweet streams, crystal springs,
above all the very nature of the place
is made for pleasure and delight …
the hills seem to laugh
and it is as if from them
gaiety emerges and
flows out …
so the entire area
can rightfully be named and
known as a paradise…
So that those who come to Florence
are amazed when they see such
things…
and so many villas all around."
L. Bruni, 'Panegirico di Firenze', c. 1420.

Florence

"… on three sides it is surrounded
by impregnable walls made by nature,
those most harsh mountains…"
G. Leti, 'Dialoghi storici', 1665.

The kestrel nests among the ruins

The owl hoots in the oak wo

"… the hills are filled with many villas…" L. Ariosto, 'Rime', 1550.
"… healthy fresh air…" L. B. Alberti, 'De re Ædificatoria', 1452.

"… full sunlight… meadows in flower and sunny fields… cool woods…

Florence

Siena

Chianti, a wine producing area between Florence and Siena:
"... most wonderfully salubrious; most fertile plains,
gentle hills, delightful groves and pleasant woods;
magnificent abundance of grain and wine and oil..."
M. Tramezzino, "I costumi", 1543.

FOR CENTURIES CHIANTI
HAS BEEN DECANTED
INTO THE TRADITIONAL
BOTTLES COVERED
WIITH STRAW; TODAY IT
IS MORE OFTEN IN
STRAIGHT GREEN WINE
BOTTLES.

"Grapes: the best
have a tender skin..."
"Tacuinum Sanitatis", 14th century.

Fiaschetteria
VINI

the correct type of glass

Adriana Morabia Silvestri was born in Milan and is a graduate of the Accademia di Brera. A graphic designer, she has also taught visual art and for nine years worked with Mondadori, one of Italy's largest publishers, as an illustrative designer. Exhibitions of her work have been held in London, New York and San Paolo; she has created artists' books exhibited in important institutions and belonging to private collections.